Copyright © 2018

All rights are reserved.

No part of this publication may be reproduced, stored in a retrieval system or transmitted in any form or by any means, electronic, mechanical, photocopying, recording or otherwise, without prior permission of the publisher.

This Book Belongs to:
....

HOW TO DRAW

If you have been looking for a book that will help you learn how to draw Anime & Manga then you have found the right book. This book is amazing for kids and adults. It is the best way to have fun together and at the same time to learn about the easier ways to draw.

Is it hard for you to get your child's attention to draw and color? Have you tried everything? Have you bought even expensive sets and still nothing? It is not about the type of colors and pencils he will use. It is about the simplicity of the lesson (Step by Step). It needs to be fun and at the same time easy to follow. That is why the drawings in this book are accepted and loved by many children in the world. Actually, adults love them too.

Every single step is shown for each drawing, even for the smallest one. But also many drawing use just simple shapes that when put together make wonderful art.

Art skills are important for every child. It helps in shaping his imagination, helps with motor skills and coordination. It is fun too.

TABLE OF CONTENTS

How To Draw :

Ash Ketchum	5
Deidara from Naruto	15
Detective Conan	25
Gaara	35
Gohan	45
Goku Super Saiyan	55
Hatsune Miku	65
Ichigo Kurosaki Bankai	75
Inuyasha	85
Itachi Uchiha	95
Kagami Hiiragi	105
Kagome Higurashi	114
Kakashi Hatake	123
Konata Izumi	133
Korra	142
Link from Legend of Zelda	152
Sasuke	162
Toshiro Hitsugaya	172

Anyone Can Draw Anime & Manga with this Book!

HOW TO DRAW: ASH KETCHUM

HOW TO DRAW: ASH KETCHUM

GRID STEP

You can draw the grid layout yourself using the following steps...
1) At the top of the sheet, determine the location of the head and draw its conditional size using an oval.
2) Draw a vertical line through the middle of the head. This will be the central vertical line of the drawing.
3) From the upper border of the head, make a mark one-sixth the height of the head. This will be the upper boundary of the figure.
4) From the top of the head, draw downward five segments equal to the height of the head.
5) From the central vertical line of the figure, measure and draw:
· One segment equal to the width of the head - to the left of the line.
· One segment equal to three-quarters the width of the head - to the left of the line.
· One segment equal to the width of the head - to the right of the line.
· One segment equal to one-third the width of the head - to the right of the line.
Through the boundaries of the segments we draw vertical lines. The extreme left and right segments are the vertical boundaries of the drawing.

HOW TO DRAW: ASH KETCHUM

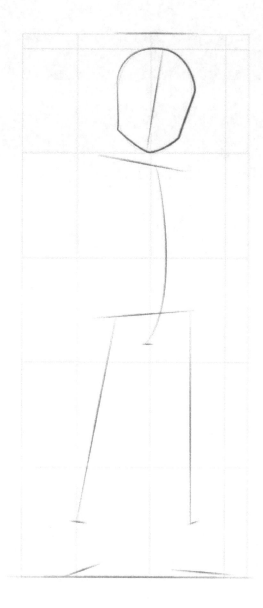

STEP 1
Mark off the width and height of the picture. Add guidelines for the body. Outline Ash's head.

HOW TO DRAW: ASH KETCHUM

STEP 2
Draw the shapes of Ash's torso and neck.

HOW TO DRAW: ASH KETCHUM

STEP 3
Define with guidelines the arms, hands, ankles and feet of the boy. Add lines for his facial features.

HOW TO DRAW: ASH KETCHUM

STEP 4
Outline the shapes of Ash Ketchum's arms, legs and cap.

HOW TO DRAW: ASH KETCHUM

STEP 5
Draw the hands, fingers, shoes. Add the cuff and the peak of the cap.

HOW TO DRAW: ASH KETCHUM

STEP 6
Add lines to the T-shirt. Draw Ash's eyes, ears and hair. Detail his cap and shoes.

HOW TO DRAW: ASH KETCHUM

STEP 7
Work on the figure, paying special attention to detail.

HOW TO DRAW: ASH KETCHUM

STEP 8
Contour Ash Ketchum, trying to vary the thickness and darkness of the line. Add more detail, add the ground. Erase all guidelines.

HOW TO DRAW: DEIDARA FROM NARUTO

HOW TO DRAW: DEIDARA FROM NARUTO

GRID STEP

You can draw the grid layout yourself using the following steps...
1) At the top of the sheet, determine the location of the head and draw its conditional size using an oval.
2) Draw a vertical line through the middle of the head. This will be the central vertical line of the drawing.
3) From the top of the head, mark one-third the height of the head. This will be the upper boundary of the figure.
4) From the upper border of the head, mark six segments equal to the height of the head and one segment equal to one-sixth the height of the head.
5) From the central vertical line of the figure, measure and draw:
· One segment equal to the width of the head – to the left of the line.
· One segment equal to two-thirds the width of the head – to the left of the line.
· Two segments equal to the width of the head – to the right of the line.
· One segment equal to half the width of the head – to the right of the line.
Through the boundaries of the segments we draw vertical lines. The extreme left and right segments are the vertical boundaries of the drawing.

HOW TO DRAW: DEIDARA FROM NARUTO

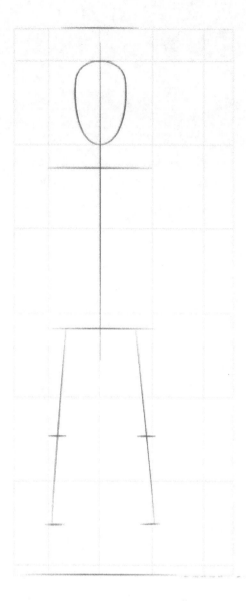

STEP 1
Mark off the width and height of the picture. Add guidelines for Deidara's body. Draw the shape of his head.

HOW TO DRAW: DEIDARA FROM NARUTO

STEP 2
Draw Deidara's body, neck and cloak.

HOW TO DRAW: DEIDARA FROM NARUTO

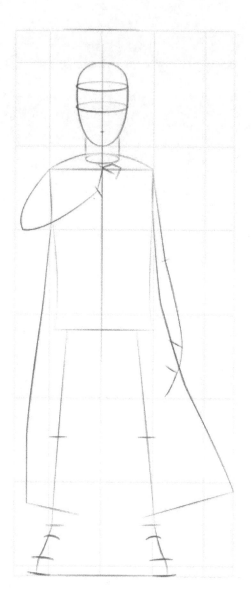

STEP 3
Add guidelines for the arms, legs and headband.

HOW TO DRAW: DEIDARA FROM NARUTO

STEP 4
Outline the shape of his sleeves, the collar, trousers and ears of the boy.

HOW TO DRAW: DEIDARA FROM NARUTO

STEP 5
Draw Deidara's hands and arms, feet, eyes and hair.

HOW TO DRAW: DEIDARA FROM NARUTO

STEP 6
Detail the clothes, lifted hand and hair.

HOW TO DRAW: DEIDARA FROM NARUTO

STEP 7
Work on the figure, paying special attention to detail.

HOW TO DRAW: DEIDARA FROM NARUTO

STEP 8
Contour Deidara, trying to vary the thickness and blackness of the line. Add more detail and add the ground. Erase all guidelines.

HOW TO DRAW: DETECTIVE CONAN

HOW TO DRAW: DETECTIVE CONAN

GRID STEP

You can draw the grid layout yourself using the following steps...
1) Draw a rectangle that will define the conditional proportions and boundaries of the chosen drawing.
2) From the middle of the rectangle, draw one vertical and one horizontal line equally dividing the shape.
3) Draw another horizontal line equally dividing the upper half of the rectangle. Similarly, draw a horizontal line equally dividing the bottom half of the rectangle.
4) Draw a vertical line equally dividing the left half of the rectangle. Similarly, draw a vertical line equally dividing the right half of the rectangle.

HOW TO DRAW: DETECTIVE CONAN

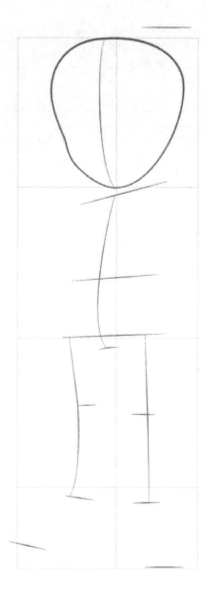

STEP 1
Mark off the width and height of the picture. Add guidelines for detective Conan's body. Draw his head. Add a line, which will act as the center of his head.

- 27 -

HOW TO DRAW: DETECTIVE CONAN

STEP 2
Draw detective Conan's body and neck.

HOW TO DRAW: DETECTIVE CONAN

STEP 3
Add guidelines for his arms, trainers and facial features.

- 29 -

HOW TO DRAW: DETECTIVE CONAN

STEP 4
Outline the left hand, legs and hair.

HOW TO DRAW: DETECTIVE CONAN

STEP 5
Draw detective Conan's arms, eyes and bow-tie. Detail his trainers.

HOW TO DRAW: DETECTIVE CONAN

STEP 6
Draw his clothes and glasses. Add his pupils, fingers of the left hand and trainers tongue.

HOW TO DRAW: DETECTIVE CONAN

STEP 7
Outline the nose. Work on the figure, paying special attention to detail.

HOW TO DRAW: DETECTIVE CONAN

STEP 8
Contour detective Conan, trying to vary the thickness and darkness of the line. Add more detail and add the grass. Erase all guidelines.

HOW TO DRAW: GAARA

HOW TO DRAW: GAARA

GRID STEP

You can draw the grid layout yourself using the following steps...
1) At the top of the sheet, determine the location of the head and draw its conditional size using an oval.
2) Draw a vertical line through the middle of the right side of the head.
3) From the upper border of the head, draw a segment equal to one-third the height of the head. This marks the upper boundary of the figure.
4) From the upper border of the head, draw seven segments equal to the height of the head and one segment equal to three-quarters the height of the head.
5) From the central vertical line of the figure, measure and draw:
· One segment equal to the width of the head – to the left of the line.
· One segment equal to two-thirds the width of the head – to the left of the line.
· Three segments of equal head width – to the right of the line.
Through the boundaries of the segments we draw vertical lines. The extreme left and right segments are the vertical boundaries of the drawing.

HOW TO DRAW: GAARA

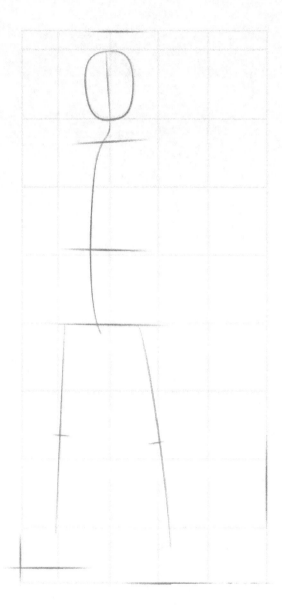

STEP 1
Mark off the width and height of the picture. Add guidelines for Gaara's body. Draw the shape of his head and draw a line through it.

HOW TO DRAW: GAARA

STEP 2
Draw Gaara's body and neck.

HOW TO DRAW: GAARA

STEP 3
Add guidelines for the guy's arms, feet and facial features.

HOW TO DRAW: GAARA

STEP 4
Outline the shapes for Gaara's arms, trousers, eyes and ears.

HOW TO DRAW: GAARA

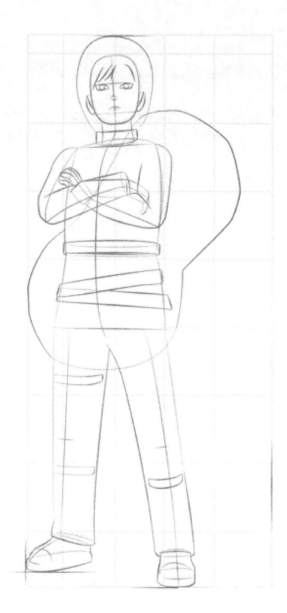

STEP 5
Draw Gaara's fingers, pupils, shoes, clothes, hair and a bag.

HOW TO DRAW: GAARA

STEP 6
Detail his hair. Add a cloak and toes. Detail the clothes, bag and eyes.

HOW TO DRAW: GAARA

STEP 7
Work on the figure, paying special attention to detail.

HOW TO DRAW: GAARA

STEP 8
Contour Gaara, trying to vary the thickness and darkness of the line. Add more detail. Erase all guidelines.

HOW TO DRAW: GOHAN

HOW TO DRAW: GOHAN

GRID STEP

You can draw the grid layout yourself using the following steps...
· At the top of the sheet, determine the location of the head and draw its approximate size, using an oval.
· Draw a vertical line through the middle of the head. This will be the central vertical line of the drawing.
· From the upper border of the head, moving upward, mark one segment equal to the height of the head. This will be the upper boundary of the figure.
· From the upper border of the head, moving downward, mark 5 segments equal to the height of the head, and one segment equal to 2/3 of the height of the head. Through the boundaries of the segments, draw horizontal lines. The last segment will act as the lower boundary of the future drawing.
· From the central vertical line of the figure, measure and draw:
- to the left of the line, one segment equal to the width of the head, plus one segment equal to 1/3 of the width of the head;
- to the right of the line, one segment equal to the width of the head, plus one segment equal to 1/2 of the width of the head.
· Draw vertical lines through the boundaries of the segments.
The extreme left and right segments are the vertical boundaries of our drawing.

HOW TO DRAW: GOHAN

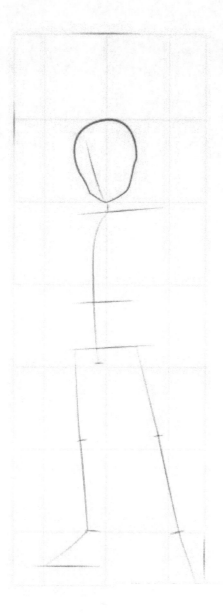

STEP 1
Mark off the width and height of the picture, and the main proportions of Gohan's figure. Draw his head and a centre line.

HOW TO DRAW: GOHAN

STEP 2
Outline his body and neck.

HOW TO DRAW: GOHAN

STEP 3
Add guidelines for the arms, feet, and proportions of Gohan's face.

- 49 -

HOW TO DRAW: GOHAN

STEP 4
Draw the shapes of the trousers, belt, and hands, as well as his eyes, ear, and nose. With smooth lines, show the general shape of his hair.

HOW TO DRAW: GOHAN

STEP 5
Sketch Gohan's hands, eyebrows, shoes, and the neck of his tunic. Draw his hair locks in detail.

HOW TO DRAW: GOHAN

STEP 6
Draw Gohan's hair, eye pupils, and fingers. Detail the shapes of his clothes.

HOW TO DRAW: GOHAN

STEP 7
Work on the whole figure, paying special attention to the details.

HOW TO DRAW: GOHAN

STEP 8
Contour Gohan, trying to vary the thickness and darkness of the line. Refine the details and add the ground. Erase all the guidelines.

HOW TO DRAW: GOKU SUPER SAIYAN

HOW TO DRAW: GOKU SUPER SAIYAN

GRID STEP

You can draw the grid layout yourself using the following steps...
1) At the top of the sheet, determine the location of the head and draw its conditional size using an oval.
2) Draw a vertical line through the middle of the head. This will be the central vertical line of the drawing.
3) From the upper border of the head, draw one segment equal to the height of the head. This will be the upper boundary of the figure.
4) From the top of the head, draw seven segments equal to the height of the head and one segment equal to half the height of the head.
5) From the central vertical line of the figure, measure and draw:
· Two segments of equal head width - to the left of the line.
· Two segments of equal head width - to the right of the line.
Through the boundaries of the segments we draw vertical lines. The extreme left and right segments are the vertical boundaries of the drawing.

HOW TO DRAW: GOKU SUPER SAIYAN

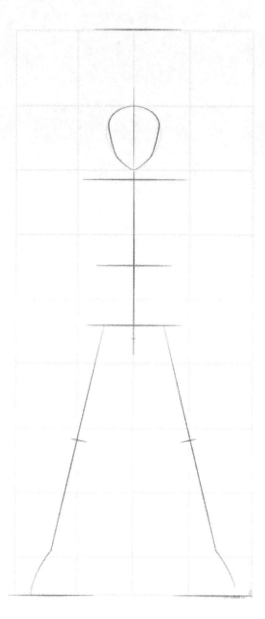

STEP 1
Mark off the width and height of the picture. Add guidelines for Goku's body. Draw his head. Add a line, which will act as the center of it.

HOW TO DRAW: GOKU SUPER SAIYAN

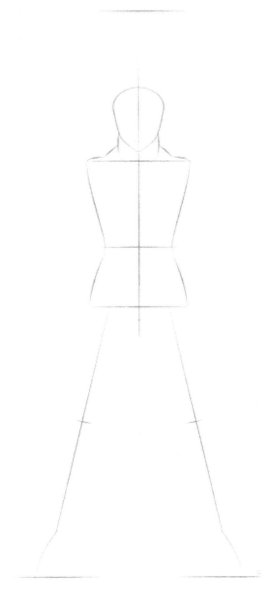

STEP 2
Draw Goku's torso and neck.

HOW TO DRAW: GOKU SUPER SAIYAN

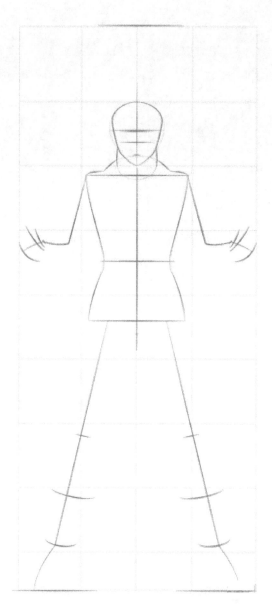

STEP 3
Add guidelines for the character's arms, legs and facial features.

HOW TO DRAW: GOKU SUPER SAIYAN

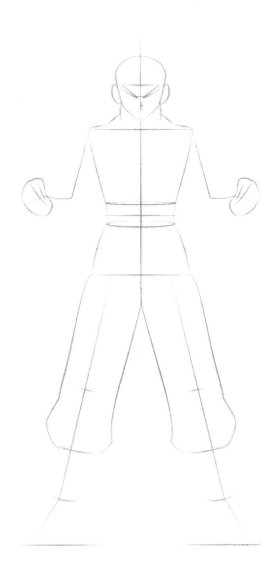

STEP 4
Outline his hands, trousers and ears. Define the place for his nose, eyebrows and belt.

HOW TO DRAW: GOKU SUPER SAIYAN

STEP 5
Sketch Goku's arms, hands, boots, hair (in general), eyes and the collar of his tunic.

HOW TO DRAW: GOKU SUPER SAIYAN

STEP 6
Draw the clothes and hair. Draw tucks on the trousers and the belt.

HOW TO DRAW: GOKU SUPER SAIYAN

STEP 7
Work on the figure, paying special attention to detail.

HOW TO DRAW: GOKU SUPER SAIYAN

STEP 8
Contour Goku from Dragon Ball Z, trying to vary the thickness and darkness of the line. Add more detail and add the floor. Erase all guidelines.

HOW TO DRAW: HATSUNE MIKU

HOW TO DRAW: HATSUNE MIKU

GRID STEP

You can draw the grid layout yourself using the following steps...
1) Draw the upper border for the figure.
2) From the upper border, moving downward, tentatively determine the position of the head and draw an oval to represent its conditional size.
3) Draw a vertical line through the middle of the head. This will be the central vertical line of the figure.
4) From the upper border of the figure, draw six identical segments equal to the height of the head and a segment equal to half the height of the head. The last segment will act as the lower boundary of the figure. Through the boundaries of the segments, draw horizontal lines.
5) From the central vertical line of the figure, measure and draw:
 · Three segments equal to the width of the head - to the left of the line.
 · Three segments equal to the width of the head - to the right of the line.
 · One segment equal to one-third the width of the head - to the right of the line.
Through the boundary of each segment, draw vertical lines. The extreme left and right segments will act as the vertical boundaries of the figure.

HOW TO DRAW: HATSUNE MIKU

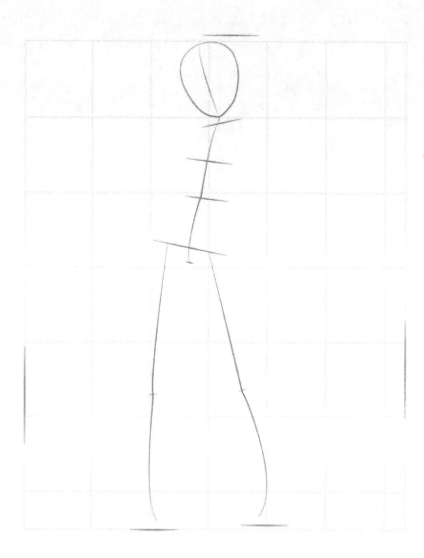

STEP 1
Mark off the width and height of Hatsune Miku. Add her head and a line through it.

HOW TO DRAW: HATSUNE MIKU

STEP 2
Draw Hatsune's neck and chest.

HOW TO DRAW: HATSUNE MIKU

STEP 3
Add guidelines for Miku's arms, legs and head.

HOW TO DRAW: HATSUNE MIKU

STEP 4
Outline the shapes of Miku's legs, arms and mouth.

HOW TO DRAW: HATSUNE MIKU

STEP 5
Add Hatsune's fingers and pupils. Sketch her hair and clothes.

HOW TO DRAW: HATSUNE MIKU

STEP 6
Draw the shapes of the hair and clothes. Add some details to the eyes.

HOW TO DRAW: HATSUNE MIKU

STEP 7
Work on the whole figure, paying special attention to detail.

HOW TO DRAW: HATSUNE MIKU

STEP 8
Contour Hatsune Miku, trying to vary the thickness and darkness of the line. Add more detail and add the floor. Erase all guidelines.

HOW TO DRAW: ICHIGO KUROSAKI BANKAI

HOW TO DRAW: ICHIGO KUROSAKI BANKAI

GRID STEP

You can draw the grid layout yourself using the following steps...
1) Draw the upper border for the figure.
2) From the upper border, moving downward, tentatively determine the position of the head and draw an oval to represent its conditional size.
3) Draw a vertical line through the middle of the head. This will be the central vertical line of the figure.
4) From the upper border of the figure, draw nine identical segments equal to the height of the head and one segment equal to one-sixth the height of the head. The last segment will act as the lower boundary of the figure. Through the boundaries of the segments, draw horizontal lines.
5) From the central vertical line of the figure, measure and draw:
· Six segments equal to the width of the head - to the left of the line.
· One segment equal to half the width of the head - to the left of the line.
· Two segments equal to the width of the head - to the right of the line.
· One segment equal to two-thirds the width of the head - to the right of the line.
Through the boundary of each segment, draw vertical lines. The extreme left and right segments will act as the vertical boundaries of the figure.

HOW TO DRAW: ICHIGO KUROSAKI BANKAI

STEP 1
Mark off the width and height of the picture. Add guidelines for Ichigo's body. Draw his head. Add a line, which will act as the center of his head.

- 77 -

HOW TO DRAW: ICHIGO KUROSAKI BANKAI

STEP 2
Draw Ichigo's torso and neck.

HOW TO DRAW: ICHIGO KUROSAKI BANKAI

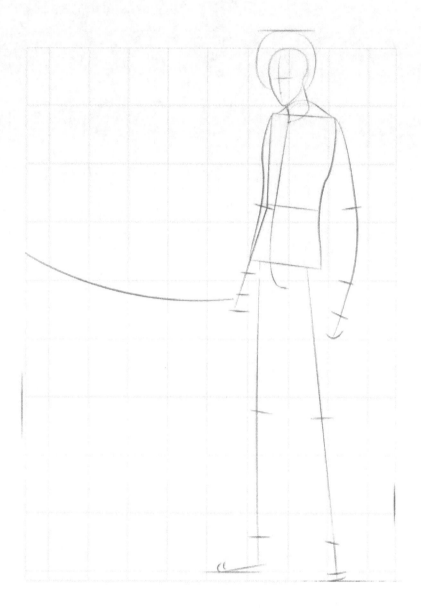

STEP 3
Add guidelines for the boy's arms, feet, hair and facial features.

HOW TO DRAW: ICHIGO KUROSAKI BANKAI

STEP 4
Outline the shapes of the arms, legs and hair.

HOW TO DRAW: ICHIGO KUROSAKI BANKAI

STEP 5
Outline Ichigo's eyes, ears, fingers, trousers and sword.

HOW TO DRAW: ICHIGO KUROSAKI BANKAI

STEP 6
Draw the rest of the clothes. Detail the shapes of Ichigo's hair and trousers.

HOW TO DRAW: ICHIGO KUROSAKI BANKAI

STEP 7
Work on the whole figure, paying special attention to detail.

HOW TO DRAW: ICHIGO KUROSAKI BANKAI

STEP 8
Contour Ichigo, trying to vary the thickness and darkness of the line. Add more detail and add the ground. Erase all guidelines.

HOW TO DRAW: INUYASHA

HOW TO DRAW: INUYASHA

GRID STEP

You can draw the grid layout yourself using the following steps…
1) At the top of the sheet, determine the location of the head and draw its conditional size using an oval.
2) Draw a vertical line through the middle of the right side of the head.
3) From the upper border of the head, draw upward a segment three-quarters the height of the head. This marks the upper boundary of the figure.
4) From the upper border of the head, draw downward six segments equal to the height of the head and one segment equal to two-thirds the height of the head.
5) From the central vertical line of the figure, measure and draw:
1. Two segments equal to the width of the head - to the left of the line.
2. One segment equal to one-third the width of the head - to the left of the line.
3. Four segments equal to the width of the head - to the right of the line.
4. One segment equal to half the width of the head - to the right of the line.
Through the boundaries of the segments we draw vertical lines. The extreme left and right segments are the vertical boundaries of the drawing.

HOW TO DRAW: INUYASHA

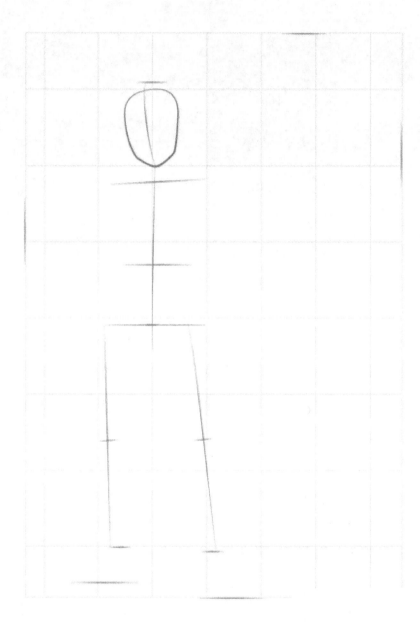

STEP 1
Mark off the width and height of the picture. Add guidelines for InuYasha's body. Draw an oval for his head. Add a line, which will act as the center his head.

HOW TO DRAW: INUYASHA

STEP 2
Draw InuYasha's torso and neck. Sketch his sword.

HOW TO DRAW: INUYASHA

STEP 3
Add guidelines for InuYasha's arms, legs and facial features.

HOW TO DRAW: INUYASHA

STEP 4
Outline the shapes of the character's sleeves, legs and sword handle. Add his eyebrows.

HOW TO DRAW: INUYASHA

STEP 5
Draw InuYasha's hands, eyes, sword and clothes.

HOW TO DRAW: INUYASHA

STEP 6
Add the fingers and toes of the character. Pay particular attention to the shape of his hair, eyes, sword and clothes.

HOW TO DRAW: INUYASHA

STEP 7
Work on the whole figure, paying special attention to detail.

HOW TO DRAW: INUYASHA

STEP 8
Contour InuYasha, trying to vary the thickness and Darkness of the line. Add more detail and add the ground. Erase all guidelines.

HOW TO DRAW: ITACHI UCHIHA

HOW TO DRAW: ITACHI UCHIHA

GRID STEP

You can draw the grid layout yourself using the following steps...
1) At the top of the sheet, determine the location of the head and draw its conditional size using an oval.
2) Draw a vertical line through the middle of the head. This will be the central vertical line of the drawing.
3) From the upper border of the head, make a mark one-third the height of the head. This is the upper boundary of the figure.
4) From the upper border of the head, draw downward six segments equal to the height of the head and one segment equal to half the height of the head.
5) From the central vertical line of the figure, measure and draw:
 · One segment equal to the width of the head - to the left of the line.
 · One segment equal to one-third the width of the head - to the left of the line.
 · One segment equal to the width of the head - to the right of the line.
 · One segment equal to half the width of the head - to the right of the line.
Through the boundaries of the segments we draw vertical lines. The extreme left and right segments are the vertical boundaries of the drawing.

HOW TO DRAW: ITACHI UCHIHA

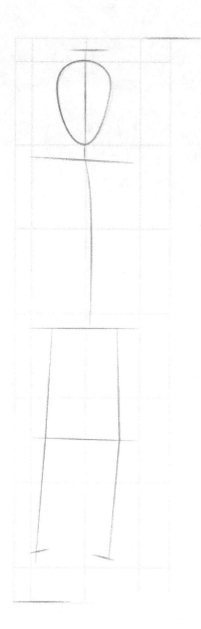

STEP 1
Mark off the width and height of the picture. Add guidelines for Itachi's body. Draw his head. Add a line, which will act as the center of his head.

HOW TO DRAW: ITACHI UCHIHA

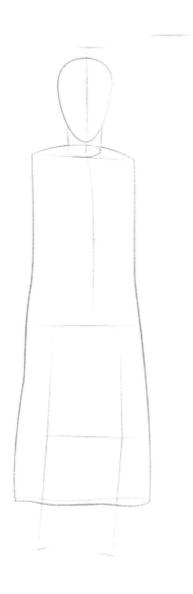

STEP 2
Draw Uchiha's neck and cloak.

HOW TO DRAW: ITACHI UCHIHA

STEP 3
Add guidelines for Itachi's arms, legs and facial features.

HOW TO DRAW: ITACHI UCHIHA

STEP 4
Outline the shapes of the sleeves, legs, hair, headband and eyes of the character.

HOW TO DRAW: ITACHI UCHIHA

STEP 5
Outline the shape of Itachi's hands, collar and shoes. Add more lines to his eyes and headband.

HOW TO DRAW: ITACHI UCHIHA

STEP 6
Add Uchiha's sword, locks and toes. Detail the shapes for the feet and clothes.

HOW TO DRAW: ITACHI UCHIHA

STEP 7
Work on the whole figure, paying special attention to detail.

HOW TO DRAW: ITACHI UCHIHA

STEP 8
Contour Itachi Uchiha, trying to vary the thickness and darkness of the line. Add more detail and add the ground. Erase all guidelines.

HOW TO DRAW: KAGAMI HIIRAGI

HOW TO DRAW: KAGAMI HIIRAGI

GRID STEP

You can draw the grid layout yourself using the following steps…
1) Draw the upper border for the figure.
2) From the upper border, moving downward, tentatively determine the position of the head and draw an oval to represent its conditional size.
3) Draw a vertical line through the middle of the head. This will be the central vertical line of the figure.
4) From the upper border of the figure, draw five identical segments equal to the height of the head. The last segment will act as the lower boundary of the figure. Through the boundaries of the segments, draw horizontal lines.
5) From the central vertical line of the figure, measure and draw:
· One segment equal to the width of the head - to the left of the line.
· One segment equal to the width of the head - to the right of the line.
Through the boundary of each segment, draw vertical lines. The extreme left and right segments will act as the vertical boundaries of the figure.

HOW TO DRAW: KAGAMI HIIRAGI

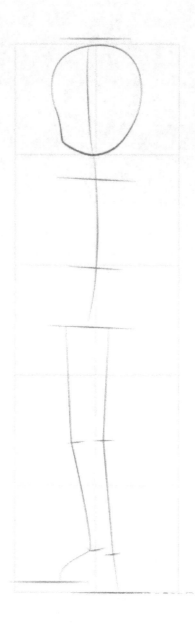

STEP 1
Mark off the width and height of Kagami. Draw the shape of her head. Add a line through the center of the figure.

HOW TO DRAW: KAGAMI HIIRAGI

STEP 2
Draw Kagami's neck, body and hair.

HOW TO DRAW: KAGAMI HIIRAGI

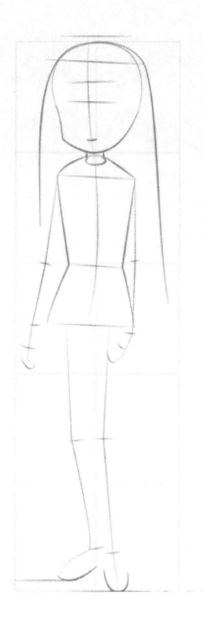

STEP 3
Draw guidelines for the girl's arms, hands, feet and facial features.

HOW TO DRAW: KAGAMI HIIRAGI

STEP 4
Add shapes for the arms, hands, legs and feet. Sketch the blouse collar.

HOW TO DRAW: KAGAMI HIIRAGI

STEP 5
Draw Kagami's fingers, clothes, irises and hair.

HOW TO DRAW: KAGAMI HIIRAGI

STEP 6
Work on the figures, paying special attention to detail.

HOW TO DRAW: KAGAMI HIIRAGI

STEP 7
Contour Kagami, trying to vary the thickness and darkness of the line. Add the ground. Erase all guidelines.

HOW TO DRAW: KAGOME HIGURASHI

HOW TO DRAW: KAGOME HIGURASHI

GRID STEP

You can draw the grid layout yourself using the following steps…
1) Draw the upper border for the figure.
2) From the upper border, moving downward, tentatively determine the position of the head and draw an oval to represent its conditional size.
3) Draw a vertical line through the middle of the head. This will be the central vertical line of the figure.
4) From the upper border of the figure, draw six identical segments equal to the height of the head and one segment equal to half the height of the head. The last segment will act as the lower boundary of the figure. Through the boundaries of the segments, draw horizontal lines.
5) From the central vertical line of the figure, measure and draw:
 · One segment equal to the width of the head – to the left of the line.
 · One segment equal to half the width of the head – to the left of the line.
 · Three segments of equal head width – to the right of the line.
Through the boundary of each segment, draw vertical lines. The extreme left and right segments will act as the vertical boundaries of the figure.

HOW TO DRAW: KAGOME HIGURASHI

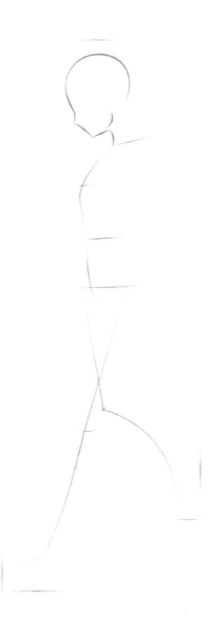

STEP 1
Mark off the width and height of the picture. Define Kagome's general proportions. Draw her head and a line through the figure.

HOW TO DRAW: KAGOME HIGURASHI

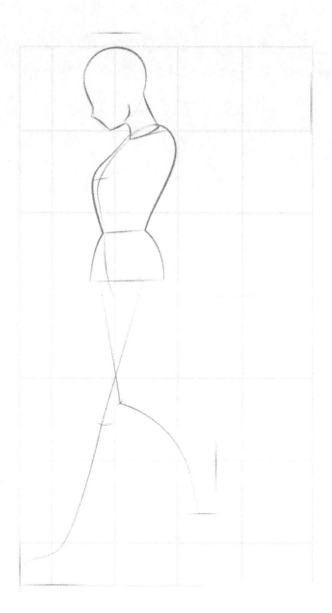

STEP 2
Draw the neck and body of the girl.

HOW TO DRAW: KAGOME HIGURASHI

STEP 3
Add guidelines for Kagome's arms, feet and facial features.

HOW TO DRAW: KAGOME HIGURASHI

STEP 4
Draw shapes for Kagome's legs, feet, arms, hair and ear.

HOW TO DRAW: KAGOME HIGURASHI

STEP 5
Sketch shapes for the clothes, hair and eye.

HOW TO DRAW: KAGOME HIGURASHI

STEP 6
Work on the figure, paying special attention to detail.

HOW TO DRAW: KAGOME HIGURASHI

STEP 7
Contour Kagome, trying to vary the thickness and darkness of the line. Add the ground. Erase all guidelines.

HOW TO DRAW: KAKASHI HATAKE

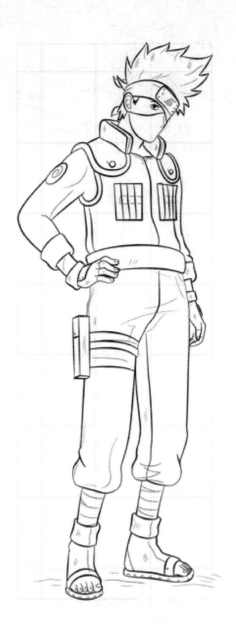

HOW TO DRAW: KAKASHI HATAKE

GRID STEP

You can draw the grid layout yourself using the following steps...
1) At the top of the sheet, determine the location of the head and draw its conditional size using an oval.
2) Draw a vertical line through the middle of the head. This will be the central vertical line of the drawing.
3) From the upper border of the head, mark a segment equal to half the height of the head. This will be the upper boundary of the figure.
4) From the top of the head, draw downward seven segments equal to the height of the head and one segment equal to half the height of the head.
5) From the central vertical line of the figure, measure and draw:
· Two segments equal to the width of the head - to the left of the line.
· One segment equal to half the width of the head - to the left of the line.
· One segment equal to the width of the head - to the right of the line.
Through the boundaries of the segments we draw vertical lines. The extreme left and right segments are the vertical boundaries of the drawing.

HOW TO DRAW: KAKASHI HATAKE

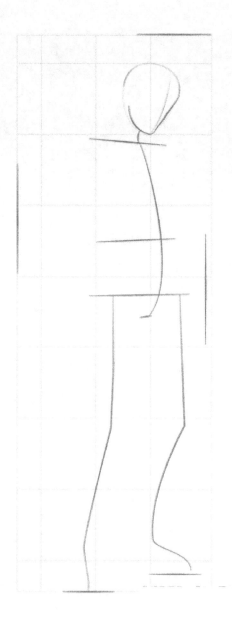

STEP 1
Mark off the width and height of the picture. Define Kakashi's general proportions. Draw his head and a line through the figure.

HOW TO DRAW: KAKASHI HATAKE

STEP 2
Draw the neck and body of the boy.

HOW TO DRAW: KAKASHI HATAKE

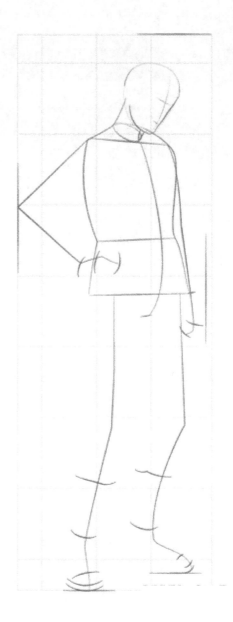

STEP 3
Add guidelines for Kakashi's arms, legs, feet and facial features.

HOW TO DRAW: KAKASHI HATAKE

STEP 4
Draw shapes for Kakashi's trousers, arms, hands, hair and ear.

HOW TO DRAW: KAKASHI HATAKE

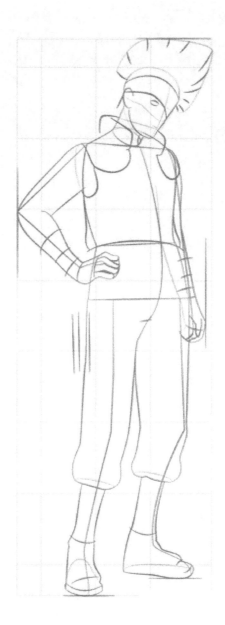

STEP 5
Sketch the shapes of the clothes, feet, fingers, hair and eye. Add the headband and parts of the jacket.

HOW TO DRAW: KAKASHI HATAKE

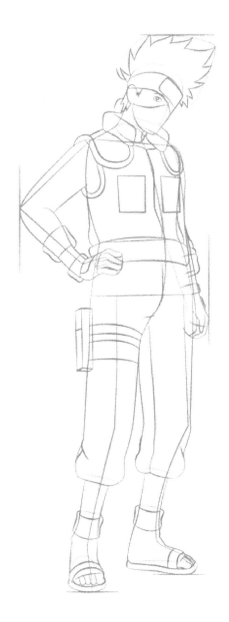

STEP 6
Add more detail to the clothes. Draw toes and hair.

HOW TO DRAW: KAKASHI HATAKE

STEP 7
Work on the figure, paying special attention to detail.

HOW TO DRAW: KAKASHI HATAKE

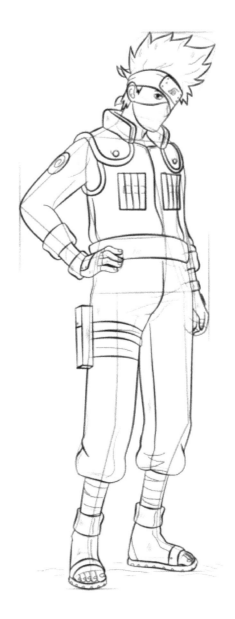

STEP 8
Contour Kakashi, trying to vary the thickness and darkness of the line. Add details. Erase all guidelines.

HOW TO DRAW: KONATA IZUMI

HOW TO DRAW: KONATA IZUMI

GRID STEP

You can draw the grid layout yourself using the following steps...
1) Draw the upper border for the figure.
2) From the upper border, moving downward, tentatively determine the position of the head and draw an oval to represent its conditional size.
3) Draw a vertical line through the middle of the right side of the head. This will be the central vertical line of the figure. The last segment will act as the lower boundary of the figure. Through the boundaries of the segments, draw horizontal lines.
4) From the upper border of the figure, draw four identical segments equal to the height of the head and one segment equal to half the height of the head.
5) From the central vertical line of the figure, measure and draw:
· Two segments equal to the width of the head - to the left of the line.
· One segment equal to the width of the head - to the right of the line.
Through the boundary of each segment, draw vertical lines. The extreme left and right segments will act as the vertical boundaries of the figure.

HOW TO DRAW: KONATA IZUMI

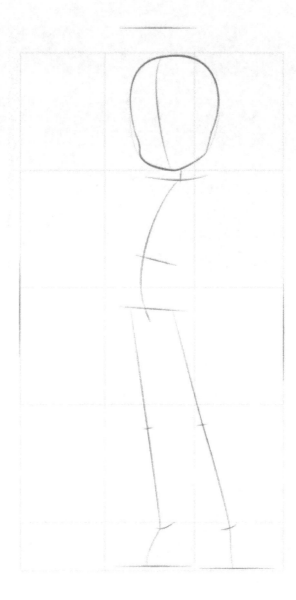

STEP 1
Mark off the width and height of the picture. Define Konata's general proportions. Draw her head and a line through her figure.

- 135 -

HOW TO DRAW: KONATA IZUMI

STEP 2
Add lines to the neck, hair and body of the girl.

HOW TO DRAW: KONATA IZUMI

STEP 3
Add guidelines for Konata's arms, hands, feet and facial features.

HOW TO DRAW: KONATA IZUMI

STEP 4
Draw the shapes of Konata's legs, feet, sleeves, eyebrows and eyes.

HOW TO DRAW: KONATA IZUMI

STEP 5
Sketch the hands, hair and clothes of the character. Add her irises.

HOW TO DRAW: KONATA IZUMI

STEP 6
Work on the figure, paying special attention to detail.

HOW TO DRAW: KONATA IZUMI

STEP 7
Contour Konata, trying to vary the thickness and darkness of the line. Add the ground. Erase all guidelines.

HOW TO DRAW: KORRA

HOW TO DRAW: KORRA

GRID STEP

You can draw the grid layout yourself using the following steps...
1) At the top of the sheet, determine the location of the head and draw its conditional size using an oval.
2) Draw a vertical line through the middle of the head. This will be the central vertical line of the drawing.
3) From the upper border of the head, make a mark one-third the height of the head. This is the upper boundary of the figure.
4) From the top of the head, draw downward seven segments equal to the height of the head and one segment equal to half the height of the head.
5) From the central vertical line of the figure, measure and draw:
· One segment equal to the width of the head - to the left of the line.
· One segment equal to half the width of the head - to the left of the line.
· Two segments equal to the width of the head - to the right of the line.
· One segment equal to half the width of the head - to the right of the line.
Through the boundaries of the segments we draw vertical lines. The extreme left and right segments are the vertical boundaries of the drawing.

HOW TO DRAW: KORRA

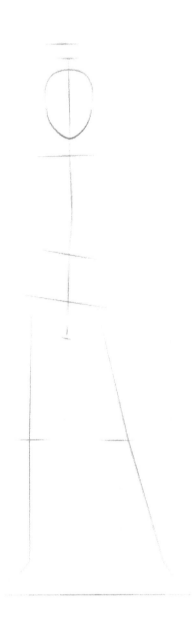

STEP 1
Mark off the width and height of the picture. Define Korra's proportions. Draw her head and a line through the figure.

HOW TO DRAW: KORRA

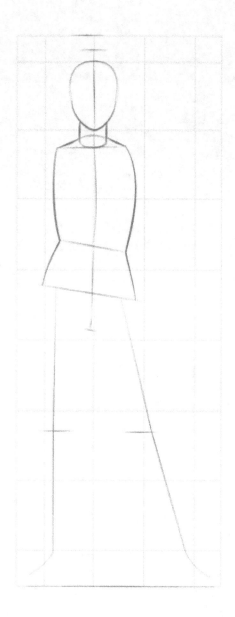

STEP 2
Draw the neck and body of the girl.

HOW TO DRAW: KORRA

STEP 3
Add guidelines for Korra's arms, hands, feet and facial features.

HOW TO DRAW: KORRA

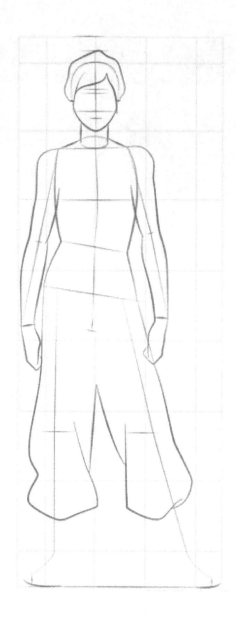

STEP 4
Draw the shapes of Korra's trousers, arms, hands and hair.

HOW TO DRAW: KORRA

STEP 5
Sketch the fingers and boots. Define places for the eyes. Work on the clothes and hair more.

HOW TO DRAW: KORRA

STEP 6
Add eyes, breasts, eyebrows, ears and clothes of the girl.

HOW TO DRAW: KORRA

STEP 7
Work on the figure, paying special attention to detail.

HOW TO DRAW: KORRA

STEP 8
Contour Korra, trying to vary the thickness and darkness of the line. Add details. Erase all guidelines.

HOW TO DRAW: LINK FROM LEGEND OF ZELDA

HOW TO DRAW: LINK FROM LEGEND OF ZELDA

GRID STEP

You can draw the grid layout yourself using the following steps...
1) Draw a rectangle that will define the conditional proportions and boundaries of the chosen drawing.
2) From the middle of the rectangle, draw one vertical and one horizontal line equally dividing the shape.
3) Draw another horizontal line equally dividing the upper half of the rectangle. Similarly, draw a horizontal line equally dividing the bottom half of the rectangle.
4) Draw a vertical line equally dividing the left half of the rectangle. Similarly, draw a vertical line equally dividing the right half of the rectangle.

HOW TO DRAW: LINK FROM LEGEND OF ZELDA

STEP 1
Mark off the width and height of the picture, as well as the main proportions of Link's figure. Draw his head, and a centre line. Draw a circle for the bird's head, and add a guideline for its beak.

HOW TO DRAW: LINK FROM LEGEND OF ZELDA

STEP 2
Outline the body and neck of Link and the bird.

HOW TO DRAW: LINK FROM LEGEND OF ZELDA

STEP 3
Draw guidelines to define where the arms and sword will be, and the proportions of Link's face. Draw a line where the centre of the bird's beak will be.

HOW TO DRAW: LINK FROM LEGEND OF ZELDA

STEP 4
Outline the shapes of the arms, legs, and sword, as well as Link's eyes and ears. Draw the eye and beak of the bird.

HOW TO DRAW: LINK FROM LEGEND OF ZELDA

STEP 5
Outline the shield, hilt, tunic, boots, belt, eye pupils, and the general shape of Link's hair. Detail the shapes of the bird's eye and head.

HOW TO DRAW: LINK FROM LEGEND OF ZELDA

STEP 6
Draw Link's hair locks, belt buckle, and fingers. Refine the shapes of the sword, shield, and the bird's crest. Add an eyelid.

HOW TO DRAW: LINK FROM LEGEND OF ZELDA

STEP 7
Detail Link's hair and clothes. Sketch the bird's wing. Work on the whole figure, paying special attention to the details.

HOW TO DRAW: LINK FROM LEGEND OF ZELDA

STEP 8
Contour, trying to vary the thickness and darkness of the line. Draw the details carefully, and add the ground. Erase all the guidelines.

HOW TO DRAW: SASUKE

HOW TO DRAW: SASUKE

GRID STEP

You can draw the grid layout yourself using the following steps...
· Draw the upper border of your drawing.
· From the upper border of the drawing, moving downward, tentatively determine the location of the head and draw its approximate size using an oval.
· Draw a vertical line through the middle of the head. This will be the central vertical line of the figure.
· From the upper border of the drawing, draw downward 6 identical segments equal to the height of the head, plus one segment equal to 3/4 of the height of the head. The last segment will act as the lower boundary of the future drawing. Draw horizontal lines through the boundaries of the segments.
· From the central vertical line of the figure, measure and draw:
- to the left of the line, 4 segments equal to the width of the head, plus one segment equal to 1/2 of the width of the head;
- to the right of the line, one segment equal to the width of the head, plus one segment equal to 2/3 of the width of the head.
· Draw vertical lines through the boundaries of the segments.
The extreme left and right segments are the vertical boundaries of your drawing.

HOW TO DRAW: SASUKE

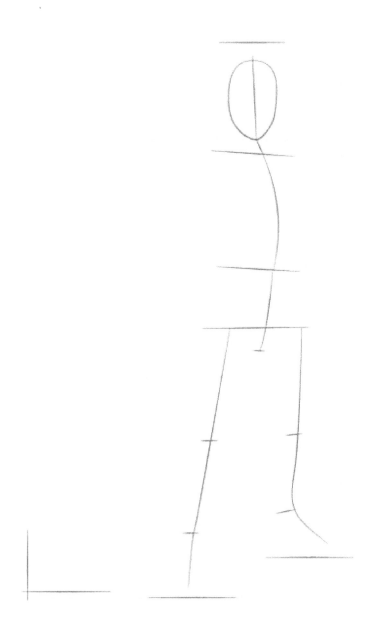

STEP 1
Mark off the width, height and main proportions of Sasuke's figure. Draw his head and a centre line.

HOW TO DRAW: SASUKE

STEP 2
Outline the torso, neck, sword, and sheath.

HOW TO DRAW: SASUKE

STEP 3
Add guidelines for his arms, legs, and the proportions of Sasuke's face.

HOW TO DRAW: SASUKE

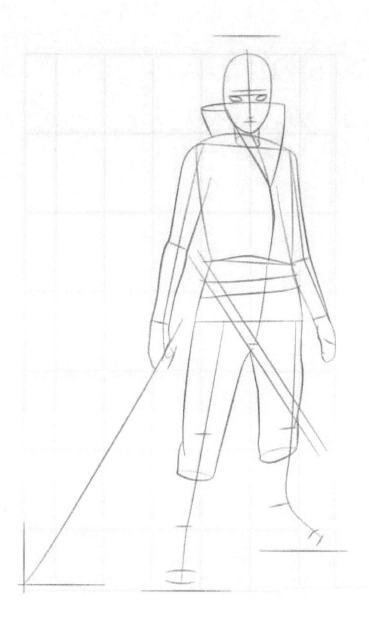

STEP 4
Draw the shapes of his arms, clothes, and eyes.

HOW TO DRAW: SASUKE

STEP 5
Draw in detail his fingers, eye pupils, legs, the general shape of his hair, sword, belt, the waist of the pants, and his braces.

HOW TO DRAW: SASUKE

STEP 6
Sketch his toes, the shapes of his clothes, and hair locks. Refine the shape of the sword.

HOW TO DRAW: SASUKE

STEP 7
Add his toenails and nose. Detail the shape of his hair and belt. Work on the whole figure, paying special attention to the details.

HOW TO DRAW: SASUKE

STEP 8
Contour Sasuke, trying to vary the thickness and darkness of the line. Draw the details more carefully, and add the ground. Erase all the guidelines.

HOW TO DRAW: TOSHIRO HITSUGAYA

HOW TO DRAW: TOSHIRO HITSUGAYA

GRID STEP

You can draw the grid layout yourself using the following steps...
1) Draw a rectangle that will define the conditional proportions and boundaries of the chosen drawing.
2) From the middle of the rectangle, draw one vertical and one horizontal line equally dividing the shape.
3) Draw another horizontal line equally dividing the upper half of the rectangle. Similarly, draw a horizontal line equally dividing the bottom half of the rectangle.
4) Draw a vertical line equally dividing the left half of the rectangle. Similarly, draw a vertical line equally dividing the right half of the rectangle.

HOW TO DRAW: TOSHIRO HITSUGAYA

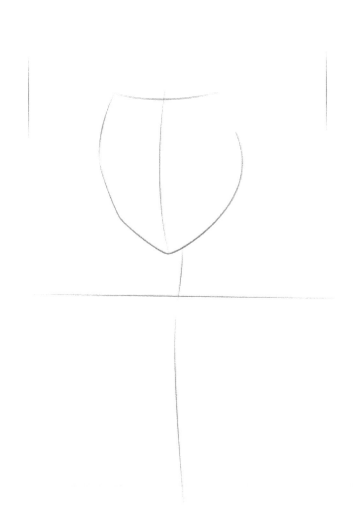

STEP 1
Mark off the width and height of the picture. Add guidelines for Toshiro's body. Draw his head. Add a line, which will act as the center of it.

HOW TO DRAW: TOSHIRO HITSUGAYA

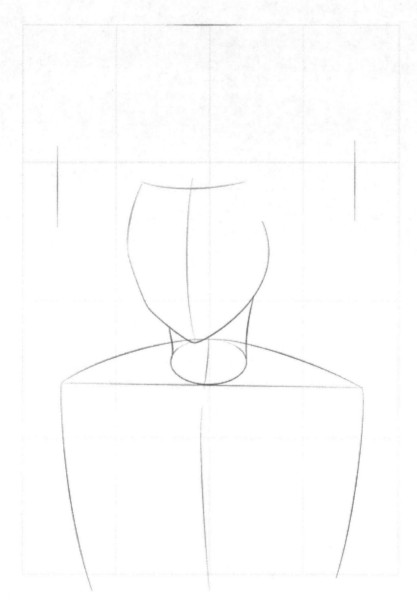

STEP 2
Draw Toshiro's torso and neck.

HOW TO DRAW: TOSHIRO HITSUGAYA

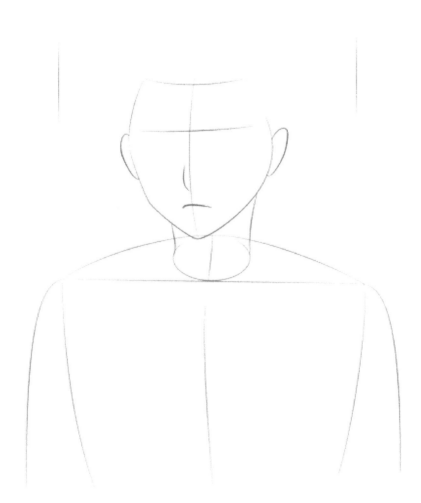

STEP 3
Add guidelines for Hitsugaya's arms, ears and facial features.

HOW TO DRAW: TOSHIRO HITSUGAYA

STEP 4
Outline the shapes of the character's clothes. Define places for his hair and eyes.

HOW TO DRAW: TOSHIRO HITSUGAYA

STEP 5
Draw Toshiro's locks and pleats on his clothes. Add his eyes.

HOW TO DRAW: TOSHIRO HITSUGAYA

STEP 6
Add more clothes. Detail the hair by adding new locks. Draw Toshiro's irises and eyebrows.

HOW TO DRAW: TOSHIRO HITSUGAYA

STEP 7
Work on the whole figure, paying special attention to detail.

HOW TO DRAW: TOSHIRO HITSUGAYA

STEP 8
Contour Toshiro Hitsugaya, trying to vary the thickness and darkness of the line. Add more detail. Erase all guidelines.

Printed in the USA
CPSIA information can be obtained
at www.ICGtesting.com
LVHW081733041224
798324LV00014BA/990